Kate Fadick

Divining

Pauletta Hansel

For Kate,
Sister-poet, fellow southerner-
May your own words be held
in my (and others') hand soon.

With love,
Pauletta

Published by WovenWord Press
811 Mapleton Ave.
Boulder, CO 80304
www.wovenword.com

ISBN: 0-9678428-7-5

"Her Words" and "Kentucky" originally appeared in *Appalachian Journal*, vol. 24, no. 3 (Spring 1997), 306-307, copyright 1997 by Appalachian State University.
The following poems first appeared in *Pine Mountain Sand and Gravel*, copyright by the Southern Appalachian Writers Cooperative: "And Then," vol. 5 (Fall 1997); "Waiting," vol. 6 (Fall 1998); "Grandpa Noah Lectures My Father on the Stars," vol. 8 (Fall 2000); and "Photograph: August 29, 1962," vol. 9 (Fall 2001).

For My Parents, Larnie and Charles Hansel, who knew these words were inside me even before I could speak them.

Acknowledgments

This book would not have been made without the help of poet Richard Hague, editor, teacher, mentor and friend. His skillful and careful attention touched every page as he divined with me the substance and shape of this work.

I am also grateful to:

❖ Mary Pierce Brosmer, founder and director of the writing school, Women Writing for (a) Change, which nurtured these words and my soul.

❖ Michael Burnham, dramaturg and director of my performance piece, *Sitting with Terry*, in which many of these poems first found voice.

❖ Julie Murray, my spiritual director.

❖ Elaine M. Prevallet SL, founding director of Knob's Haven Retreat Center at the Sisters of Loretto Motherhouse in Nerinx, Kentucky, my holy ground.

❖ My teachers and mentors over the years: M. Joe Eaton, Bob Snyder, George Ella Lyon, Jim Wayne Miller, Joe Enzweiler and John Ray.

❖ My many writing friends who helped craft the poems this book contains.

The development and publication of this book were funded in part by grants from the City of Cincinnati. Thanks to the members and staff of the City's Arts Allocation Committee for their arts advocacy and for their selection of this project for funding.

Contents

Foreword

When she was fifteen and living in Eastern Kentucky, Pauletta Hansel was interviewed for an article on Appalachian women poets which appeared in *Ms. Magazine*. A year after this remarkably precocious national exposure she dropped out of high school, under-challenged, restless with adolescence and poetry. Still diploma-less, she enrolled in Antioch College's Appalachian campus at Beckley, West Virginia, where three years later she became its last graduate. While there, she co-founded and named the Soupbean Poets, a politically active writers' group mentored by Antioch Appalachia faculty P. J. Laska and Bob Snyder. At the same time she helped establish the Southern Appalachian Writers Cooperative, which continues to support and publish contemporary Appalachian writing. But by the time of the publication, almost two decades later, of some of Hansel's early poems in *Old Wounds, New Words*, edited by Bob Henry Baber, George Ella Lyon, and Gurney Norman, and published by the Jesse Stuart Foundation, Hansel had fallen into a silence that had lasted a decade; since 1984 she had she hardly written a thing. In part, she says, her discomfort with being classified an "Appalachian poet" contributed to her silence.

A couple of turnings in her life around 1994 led to the recovery of her voice. She began to attend a writer's support group and workshop called Women Writing for (a) Change in Cincinnati. Directed by Mary Pierce Brosmer, the workshop offered women a place to work among other women in an atmosphere free from criticism and competition. Journal entries came first, then the poems began to return, including "Her Words," "Houses," and "Kentucky." Then, in 1996, Hansel volunteered to attend to the dying Terry Flanigan, a man she had been casually acquainted following her days of performing with the populist theater group Street Talk in Cincinnati. She sat with Terry every Tuesday night; the vigil lasted for more than six months until his death in August, 1996.

In order to deal with the many issues Flanigan's protracted suffering raised in her, Hansel began to write about the experience. In 1998 a suite of poems, journal entries, dreams, and monologues became *Sitting With Terry*, a one-woman performance piece from which many of the poems in the third section of *Divining* come. Through the working out of her own and Flanigan's suffering, and the coming to terms with the memories and regrets the suffering dredged up, her poems slowly took form.

Not surprisingly, the motif of death and rebirth is one of the several threads running through *Divining*. Hansel's own silence was a kind of death, and her recovery of her voice as a writer is one of the book's strengths. The serious pun of the title suggests not only unusual knowledge or insight, connected with the magical act of finding water with divining rods in rural areas, but also the divining of mystery—here, most specifically the mysteries of death, family, Self. The title also suggests the redemptive resurrection of the soul, transformed in the cauldrons of memory and suffering. The Terry poems are a kind of verbal Pieta, in which the sensibilities of the troubled and loving poet attempt to divine the meaning of his death, and simultaneously to divine the direction of her own life. Yet another part of the meaning of the title and the poems is the sacralizing of experience: in all of the poems there is an acknowledgment of the importance of daily acts and of relationships, between friends, lovers, family members, and between the individual and her place—her house, home, region, and her history. To write is to discern and express these relationships—to divine their meaning, and to articulate their transcendent significance.

These poems are as personal as poems can get, yet they read like the stories of ourselves or our loved ones. We will recognize sister, mother, father, brother, maiden aunt, gruff neighbor, and the uncertain Self, always struggling to approach the divinity of life and death. The poems contemplate life from a sober and hardheaded realism. Admirably, they rarely resolve the tensions and conflicts at their centers—they realize, and continue to love, the fallen world we have been given. They are a record, restrained, keeping their own distance, of the soul of their writer. We witness in them an honesty and forthrightness and candor which, perhaps, only poetry can bring us so briefly yet so powerfully. Most importantly, they remind us of the habits of heart and spirit without which our own souls might perish.

©Richard Hague, June 2000

Divining

There is nothing
I've ever loved—
no one

in whom I could not find
a vein of grief,
sometimes just below

the smooth and
glossy surface.
I lightly rest my hand,

feel it pulsing
hot and liquid
up against the

hollow of my palm.
I know just
where I am.

What She Carried

Writing Lessons

(I.)

I look for the way
things will turn
out

Poetics, *A.R. Ammons*

I am trying to find the shape of things,
to find where words might go
without the prodding of my pen,
left to their own devices:
startled sidling up
as if unnoticed,
nestling in the curve
of *century's* end;
places I have never seen—
Niagara Falls, Lookout Mountain—
sliding down
between the floorboards
of my mother's kitchen, 1962.

I am trying to find the shape of things,
to let them unfold
without my restless hands forever
moving, pressing up or down
into the patterns
so familiar they are all I ever
dare to sew;
to let this life unfold:
a bolt of cloth spilling
from a tall shelf,
haphazard by its own design;
a liar's yarn spinning out
incredulously true.

Photograph: August 29, 1962

It is my birthday; I am three
years old and my mother leans
down into the frame to join me
in her harlequin glasses

and striped shirtwaist dress
she sewed up just like mine.
She is holding a tray,
tin-foil and cardboard

with a teddy-bear cake,
chocolate and coconut fur,
she has baked just for me.
My hair is the color of new sand.

My mother is smiling;
someone else is taking
the picture for once;
maybe my father

grins back from behind the lens.
The photo is faded,
the edges frayed
as if it has been taken

from the album too many times
and held in a small palm.
I am smiling, too,
but not for the camera

or for anyone but my own
young self in my soft striped
dress like my mother's,
smiling that smile like

an arc which begins and
ends inside me and is
pleased to take in
anyone who happens in its path.

Kentucky

I am from there.
My roots spread wide under mountains,
rising to touch surface of earth
in towns now eroded,
their people washed north
in a great flood of hope
and despair.
I am from places with names hard in my mouth:
Seco, Hazard, Yeaddiss.
I am from the mouth of Cutshin Creek,
the last house at the head of the holler
where my mother was born.
It's gone now,
her grandfather's land sold
down to the very last acre:
half dollar an acre
put food on the table
that year.
I am from every town my father found a job
he thought would last.
I am from the pages of the books
he carried with him.
I am from all the gardens my mother never planted.
I am from kudzu and coal,
from too much and too little.
I am from there.

Her Words

Each Saturday her father Noah
was at home
she'd best stay gone till dark,
the oil lamp's light
too dim
for him to write his letters then,
and Sunday the Lord's day:
safe from all
but work and prayer.

Some Saturdays he'd catch her,
a shadow past the corner of his eye,
and draw her back,
bring out the ink and pen
to write again to Matthew
over the hill in Harlan.
Dear Friend,
the corn crop's in,
no rain since Sunday week,
I hope this finds you well.

Each word he'd speak,
she'd spell,
he'd write that word,
a slow stiff scrawl,
then lift the pen up from the page
and speak again
and on and on,
meanwhile, her own words
stuffed too far
back in her throat
like acorns stored for winter
then forgotten.

What would they have been,
my mother's words,
had they been hers to write?
Sycamore,
muslin,
blackberry,
crow:
rich and pungent on her tongue,
the sweet round vowels and jagged consonants
dropped down on the page like nut shells
at the bottom of a tree.

When I was five I wrote a book
of poems and little stories,
long since lost.
I'd pull out paper,
thick and waxy crayons,
and sit down at my mother's feet.

I'd speak the word,
she'd spell,
I'd write
and never know
her words
pushed harsh against her throat
as time collapsed and there she sat
watching her father's hand
move slow and awkward
on the page.
She'd swallow hard,
spell the word,
wait silent for the next.

What She Carried

I keep thinking about that watermelon,
the one you carried
two miles from the store
and up the holler
for his birthday,
July 4, same as the nation's—
that's the way your uncle
Dewey remembered.
He told you, "Take a melon
for your daddy
when you go."

He'd been drinking, your father,
or maybe only
drunk with rage,
his anger all
you ever could be sure of.
He grabbed the melon
up from your triumphant arms
and dashed it to the ground
(money wasted, foolish children.)
You fixed him
with eyes black as his
and never told him,
then or ever,
that you'd not spent his coins.

Was he sorry, later,
when he knew?
It didn't matter,
then or ever,
not to you.

I keep thinking of those seeds
that you carried,
in that melon,
black as eyes.
I see you
reach down to the ground,
pick up three
and place them
underneath your tongue,
one for each of us,
your children:
seeds of silence, rage.

My Mother, Not Yet Forty

In all the photographs of you
in those, my middle childhood years,
you are caught mid-word,
instructing whichever one of us
it is who holds the camera—
No, the other button, there.
You want to grab the camera,
saying— *Here, like this,*
I'll do it,
you go on,
I just don't have this time
to stop
and let you see me.

And we never did
see you
any more than we saw
the doors we walked through—
you let us in
and out.

As for me, your middle child,
in photographs of me
in those, your middle years,
I am sitting very still,
my arms tight against
my growing body—
I would hold it back,
if I could,
I would be invisible if that is what
you need from me.
If I can, I will.

I do not know where you went
in those years,
in that long dark corridor of time
of my father's depression—
it sat beside him
in his chair as he slept;
we crept around them both
as not to wake them up
too soon.

You could not help him,
you could never
make him happy, then,
and I could not make you happy:
it was never
enough,
I couldn't do it fast
enough,
I am not good
enough.
I don't know what you want.
I can't be who you are.

Sometimes I'd study
pictures of the girl
who would be my mother.
She sat so still,
her hands and ankles crossed,
a smile just behind her lips,
your lips,
like mine.
How did she
become you,
and will I
become you too?

I do not know where I went,
in those years
my body growing softer, round
like yours;
inside that body—
shell of flesh—
I was there,
quietly breathing.

Spite

When her brother died—
Jimmy, the first one,
nearly 60 years
before the rest began to fall,
each in his own year,
as they were born, like stair steps,
death missing my mother's rung—

her father brought a stone
up from the creek,
five sharp nails
from a bin in the shed.
He'd carve the name himself,
and have her spell,
her finger her nail

as she scratched first the "J"
in the pebbled dirt by the grave,
and he'd copy, or try to:
with every mistake he'd
rasp smooth the
surface of stone,
and start again.

Was this love?
As close as he ever came
to love in these stories
she tells me now:
this stone his only gift,
this name the only one
he ever spoke without demand.

I try to see her there,
hard habit of her mouth—
even her dead brother's name
she could not say to him with love,
even the cold round stone of grief
lodged between throat and voice
she would not give him.

My Father's God

(A Preacher's Daughter)

It isn't that I've not believed in God,
it's just been hard for me to think
He really mattered,
to think Him not superfluous
as most men in my life,
hovering at its margins
with their vague and useless
promises of love.

And if God is the Father,
let's start there with my father,
how he could barely leave his chair,
weighted down by his despair,
almost visibly astride him,
almost luminous in his long nights,
like the tip of his cigarette.
We knew he was still breathing
by his sharp intake of light.

Oh, my daddy loved me,
this I know,
and never doubted.
It billowed out from him
like clouds of smoke, but
what did his love matter
when he never got up from his chair
and danced me on his toes again,
after his daddy died?

And if God was his Father
why must he sit there unprotected,
yet surrounded by his icons
and his holy books of promises and prayer?

Had he turned his face from God then,
or was he turned completely to Him?
I never could decide,
but knew I wanted no part
of my father's God,
demanding all
and giving nothing
in return, that I could ever see.
And I have given that God nothing,
but let Him hover there, ignored.
I think He's waiting still,
but I am never sure.

Grandpa Noah Lectures My Father on the Stars

I wish I could have been there
but I wasn't anywhere as yet,
not even a name for me
as there was then for my sister—
Renee, *rebirth*—
herself three years unborn
when my mother's father
lectured her knobby-boned
and book-learned suitor
on the stars.

They would not have touched,
no calloused hand on
my father's thin shoulder,
but drifted,
each in his own orbit,
as Noah spoke what might have been
his only poetry in words.

I would have liked to hear those words,
what message lay between them
as he handed to his oldest daughter's lover
the knowledge of a world
beyond the coal-filled earth
once passed to him.

I know, because he told me,
my father never did accept
this gift of sky, and even now,
five decades later,
just the thought of Noah knowing

constellations, planets, navigation by the stars,
never having read a book or even
heard the word astronomy,
curls my father's lip.
But he did.

I know because my mother tells me
how her father traveled distances
only at night—
no stranger in a land
on which the stars still shone.

He was not a good man,
Noah, nor a wise one:
there are many tales, half-told,
that make my mother's eyes go dark
before she's through.
I know this marriage was
for her, and for my father too,
their own rebirthing of themselves
into a life uncharted
by stars or seasons,
or geography of birth.

Still, I would have liked to hear
this lecture on the stars,
hear for myself
this lesson Grandpa Noah
chose to have remembered,
now forgotten
as I guide my feet along this earth.

Sight

When he tells me
for the eighteenth time,
at least,
in just as many years,
I grow more beautiful
each visit home,
I know,
as I always do,
he means each year
I look more like my mother—
hair turning grey,
skin growing softer
on the bone.

I smile and say
he must be seeing me
with his Welsh
grandma's
second sight.

And it is true
there is another lens
my father uses on me—
sees my mother
at my age,
and me
the age that I was
then,
and in the year
I first left home.
He sees my mother now;
he sees the woman I'll be
when he's gone—
all layered on my face.

I'll wear those faces
for his sake
and for the look
that comes into his eyes.
I hold that picture
of him
now;
I'll find it later
layered there
among the others
just beyond my sight.

My Mother's Garden

There are no gardens
in that patch of shade I hold inside
that is my childhood,
only silk and plastic flowers in a bowl,
a single rose bush
in a hard baked front yard.

She told me
she knew the names of trees once,
and which berries she could eat
and which would stain her doll's lips red
like blood around a closing wound.
She had no use for gardens now.
She'd spent her own dark patch
of childhood hoeing, weeding,
working rows of beans, of corn,
of sisters, brothers given to her care:
of anything both brave
and fool enough to grow in that harsh land.

Gardening for food was survival,
the only kind she knew
and swore she'd never need again.
Gardening for beauty,
a luxury she thought never to afford.
Grown now, she made our home
between those ends.

When did she know
she carried all those gardens in her
like seeds kept cool and dormant,
safe even from her own desire?

One year shy of sixty
she planted her first garden
in her own bright patch of land:
aster and allium,
sweet william and zinnia.
Forty years of gardens
broke through my mother's earth.
In soft damp dusk
she worked it on her knees:
cracked red clay
grew rich and sweet as blood,
streaked up her arms
and wiped across her brow.
There was no part of her
that did not ache.
There was no part of her
that did not at last
rise up to sun and rain.

For these past years
she's sown the seeds she held,
dug beds that can't contain her.
New gardens grow from bouquets tossed away,
spilling out onto the road
and up between the jagged cracks of sidewalk—
there is not land enough
to hold my mother's garden.

Photograph: Easter Sunday, 1965

The snow
at last has thawed, the world is mud
and sidewalk; we are walking home
from church.

I am six, the parking meters taller
than me still.
I am in clothes my mother
made for me to wear this day:
my red jumper, stiff velveteen
against my skin,
over this, a grey cloth coat,
unbuttoned.

I know my mother
holds the camera,
I know she has me
in her frame.
My left arm out for balance,
I am placing one careful foot to the other,
patent leather heel to toe
as if walking on a ledge
that only I can see.

Underneath the mud,
blades of grass and crocus stir,
restless with spring.

Houses

Houses

Within the wheel of the zodiac
there are twelve houses.
Women born in the twelfth house
lose their fathers early
through death of body,
death of spirit.
Throughout their lives
their homes are haunted.
They marry late
or not at all.
They seek to marry God.

I lost my father
the year he lost his God,
the year his father,
lost to him from birth,
at long last died
and took my father's final hope
of resurrection
as beloved son.

My father never knew
he walked this ledge of hope
until he landed
twisted in his middle years
to find himself
a boy alone
and without faith
enough to find his God
in wife or children.
We lost him then,
for a time.
I was five.

I have lived
in many houses.
In this one
now
I live alone.
I seek my God
in the soil of my garden,
in the books that line my walls
as they line the walls of my father's home,
in this life I weave
of work and friends and solitude.

It is a good house
and it is haunted
by the life I have not lived
in some other house
beside a man who finds
his God in me
as I find mine in him.
Sometimes I dream this life.
Sometimes
I dream I walk along a ledge
just wide enough
for me alone.

Reflections

There are some people
who want to tell you everything,
especially what hurts—
bones splintered in childhood,
shards of ice
left inside a woman's heart
by the one who held her first,
even the small
quick slap of words
from the grocer that day,
or maybe the day before,
over egg shells
shattered, or small change.
They don't want to hear
any of yours,
except perhaps to compare,
safely righteous in their own.

I see them coming,
catch them
from the corner of my eye,
as if reflections
from a broken pane of glass
from a window in a house
I lived in once,
in a town I thought
was far from here
yet

there I am.

Old Maids

An old maid of twenty-five,
she lived next door
when I was nine,
Maxine
with her beehive hair,
make-up
and boyfriends,
come north to work
in an office,
find a man.

It was the Sixties, after all:
each year
her hair got softer,
eyes grew harder,
desperation lacquered into place.
I'd overhear what I could not understand
but knew I'd best not ask:
how a married man
could be her boyfriend, too,
and what it was, the one thing
and the one thing only,
these men wanted?

I was well into my thirties
before I became an old maid, too.
And even though I'd been too young
to learn the things
she could have taught me
in those years—
how hair spray and nail polish
can harden into place
almost any surface you might

show the world—
what I had understood was this:
(even without the words
to name it then)
I'd seen a shame in being single,
a shame in wanting
what is not yours to have.

She

That spring
she let herself go,
uncoiled the cord
and slipped out through
the crack in the window.

She was unleashed.
Even her hair sprung
free of curl.
Her clothes
would not stay put.

She spoke too loudly.
Sentences ran on
ahead of her.
She followed
when she chose.

When people said
they didn't know her
anymore,
she did not
hear them.

Night Words

I wish I could remember
the poem I got in bed with
last night—
he grabbed my wrist
just before the tables
were wiped clean
and doors propped open
urging exit
through the night.
I let him
pull me up
and lay me down.

All night
in tangled dreams,
he held me—
even as day's sharp
elbow pushed me near
to outer edge of sleep,
even as damp night
breathed me safe
back in.

This morning
only shadow stayed,
like ghost words
on the sheet of paper
underneath the one
which held the pattern
of my pen,
soon smoothed away.

Why I Write

This is the only way I know
to appease my heart—
that foolhardy muscle,
pacing its ventricled cage.

It is as greedy as any
part of me,
not content with scraps
from what my eyes devour.

I think it breaks free
of me as I sleep
and roams the back alleys
of other dreamers' dreams.

It wants to touch the insides of things.
It will split itself open
and me
and you, as well,

if it can find
no other way inside.
It wants even more of you
than I do.

June

Some summer nights
I feel I'm barely
tethered to this earth.

I am in bed
too soon,
night is scarcely darkened.

The sheet's too thin:
it cannot hold
me to this here, this now.

I think that I should
rise to bolt
windows and the door

or sometime before
morning
I may float away.

Tonight the air is heavy
with the rain
sodden earth no longer holds.

The air, the earth,
one takes
what the other

does not need.
I hover here
between the two,

unclaimed.

What I Need

I need the white space
between the lines,
that sinking-down
between the words;

a good metaphor
to write my life around.
Some days
house will do,

four walls built
brick by solid brick,
undone:
the turning of the seasons

seeping up
from underneath—
crumbling mortar
letting in the spring.

What do I need?
I need a quiet room,
or a noisy one,
my thoughts pushed down

beneath its clamor
and squeezed out onto
whatever page
I find at hand.

No room at all—
a tree stump,
a hard damp piece
of ground.

Stranger

You come into my house
smelling of rock,
snow,

things I haven't chosen
for myself.
I take you in.

You eat up all my food,
the cupboards
cannot hold enough to feed

your hunger like a cavern
open to the belly of a world
to which I do not go.

You trail in dirt.
I do not know this house
with you inside;

it's springing leaks,
the roof seams
sigh, wrench apart—

I am laid open to the sky.

Where The Dead Go

(To Terry Flanigan, 1952-1996)

Waking Before Dark

Waking up and then remembering
you are dying
must be like waking
before dark,
believing it is morning;
but in the thickening shadows you can see
the day behind, and you close
your eyes again, try to recall:
Was it a good day?
What did I do
with it?
Who did I hold?
Was it enough?
Was I?

It is slipping away, this day,
you have been sleeping,
you don't know how long
you've been sleeping,
but you want it back,
if not the life,
at least that half breath between there
and here, when it was morning
and you could believe
there's always more.

I Stood There

I stood there thinking
it was funny, almost,
that the first penis I would see in,
I don't know,
half a decade, maybe,
would be yours,
which I would never see
if you were up and
walking down the street,
black leather and
chains, like maybe you were
rough trade,
and not chained to this bed
by your sad tired dick
pissing in a tube.
I would have told you.
You might have laughed
the loudest
as you always did
before,
but it was more than I could do
to stand there
talking about dicks
and whose I had or hadn't seen
while I watched your lover
wash yours.

And Then

For John Ray

At first everything makes you think of him:
street corners, houses,
rooms you entered together,
pictures of the far-off lands

you meant to see, someday,
even your own silent, sacred places
you enter alone as if naked and holy—
those remind you, too.

They are hard and bright as precious stones,
these first days after death,
when you must hold him still,
before he fades into the years.

What's lost first
after his body, sent to be ashes
weeks ago?
Will you lose the bitter smell of him,

the press of his bones
against your own,
or the crow of his laugh
shot across the room?

Or some tiny fragment of your past
you can't recall: *What is the name of that town?*
We stayed there in the fall. I never can
remember. And you turn to hear his answer . . .

One by one they go,
the pieces of your life
he held fast for you both,
like the last remains of childhood

thrown away one spring
when you'd been gone too long
to call that place home: a river rock,
a turtle shell left crumbling in its box.

If I Ever

If I ever make a movie about war,
there will be no death

without a story,
no life a sprawling body on a field.

It would be too long, I know,
this movie about war

where every body has a mother
and a turtle or a cat.

He broke his leg when he was seven,
and his sister called him names.

In school he hated science, could not bear
to slice into a beating heart.

And now his girl proclaims his feet
too cold in winter,

but forbids him socks in bed:
she will warm them here

between her own,
shivering in his arms.

No one would want to watch
when every bullet breaking bone

begins a life told backwards,
death to birth.

After Death
(Swimming Lessons)

Tuesday, 5:15, I sink
down into this shivering pool,
my mind holding you
both live and dead,
as if in two hands weighing.

On Tuesdays I can believe
you're waiting for me still,
in your dark room,
floating
in your narrow bed,
half-dreaming

you are walking
down some familiar street,
until I come and take your hand,
pulling you back
through cold grey metal bars
into your bed.

My hand smells of chlorine,
supper,
my life beyond this room,
the last container of your life—
smelling only of death.
Your death.

In my other hand,
now cupping water,
I hold that other Tuesday,
sinking down in this pool
as you, in your dark room,
pushed out that last sweet breath,

the one you'd held since your beginning,
sucked in with your first angry cry.
I moved through water then
as now, thinking of you waiting,
not knowing I would walk into that room
and take your empty hand.

Tuesday, 5:15,
I move back and forth through water,
touching one cold hard wall
and then the other.

Dream

Startled from sleep at 6 am—
still dark and darker
still tomorrow,
December mornings slipping
toward the longest night.

It was maybe a raccoon or possum,
some sly creature of the night—
a racket in the basement.
I am jolted up through thin
membrane of dream into my room.

It was a dream of babies.
I was charged, somehow,
with caring for two lives,
their bird-bone feet
and shiny cat-like eyes,

and one their father loved,
but not the other,
as I held both out to him.
Then I broke
through sleep and thought:

That was a dream of Terry!
though he died last summer,
forty-three and not a baby,
one frail man
now bone and ash.

All spring I sat beside his bed
and rubbed his twisted feet,
those feet
that would not learn
again to touch the ground.

And now all day I ask—
was he the one beloved
or the other?
If I had stayed below the surface
was there more that I could do?

Could I have earned that love
for both, not one,
and passed them then into
their father's hands
and walked away?

The Cuckoo's Gift

It's not a fair comparison, I know,
neither elegant nor just:
you, a dead man, to a cuckoo,
one of those birds, bold and raucous,
that plant their eggs in sparrows' nests
and fly away.

You didn't choose to die
or even know that I would be the one
to shelter him when he was
folded up in grief.
He was so small and lost,
my heart span wide enough

to hold him then,
the shadow of your dying over us.
I didn't know he'd grow so large.
I didn't know my sparrow heart
would soon be filled and stretched
and pulled wide open

just to hold a dead man's lover
long enough
to let him go.

On Our Own Soil

Two months before you died
you told me your dream—
all the world's armies invading Cincinnati.
Hour upon hour, another nation joins the fight,
the sky dark with jet bombers,
the freeways clogged with tanks,
the river red and swollen with the bodies
first to fall.

You were home in your dream
in that house on Victor,
pacing narrow halls
and narrow choices:

Stay,
save your friends, if you can,
plot a fine resistance.
Flee,
save yourself,
you know the places you can hide
until whatever end might come.

What did you choose, I ask,
waiting there beside your bed
so long I think you might be dreaming once again . . .
I don't know.

And I didn't know—
which question did I ask,
which question did you answer?
Here is what I know today:
you stayed
as long as you could

and we were your army,
your front line, your resistance.
We were not enough.
You're safe now;
how can we not be glad for you,
but you have left us
veterans
of this futile war
from which we never can return,
this war on our own soil.

Where the Dead Go

For awhile after he died,
a year
maybe more,
in my dreams
nothing could stay dead.
I was forever
coming to them, dead,

bringing them to life.
It started quite specifically—
his lover,
my parents,
the cats in my bed—
all the fragile beating hearts
I carried in my own.

Night after night,
death after death,
I'd bring them back,
broken and scarred,
but living,
rising from coffins or concrete
before dawn.

Then it was strangers
I'd save,
their deaths
brutal and fast.
From my window I'd watch
as bullets broke bone,
bodies pitched down into dirt.

Sometime near waking
I'd walk out through the night,

gather green shoots
from the ground
where they fell,
knowing by day
they'd grow back into men.

Once
I was the one who died,
slipping down below
the surface of black water
where all the dead go,
carrying with them
the cold hollow places

they died with
forever.
This is the difference
between living and death,
they told me,
the ones who had
fallen before:

as long as you live
what is shattered inside you
can heal.
And was that the night I knew
I must rise up
through that cold dark
knowledge of death?

Was that the night I knew,
finally,
just who it was
I needed to make live?

Waiting

There is a moment
when it changes.
I have been traveling,
let's say, by air,
a constant forward motion,
and to the east,
clouds,
and to the west
the sun is at last setting.

We have been flying
into the sun for hours,
it seems,
and now it is setting
finally on this day which began
somewhere else,
will end
some place I have not seen.

And then I have almost forgotten
that place it began.
I have almost forgotten where
I am going,
or even that I am going
anywhere at all.

Why am I
thinking of you, now,
in your final weeks?
In the setting sun
I would sit by your bed,
full, at first,
of where I had been,
where I would go.

I was waiting then,
we all were waiting,
it seems,
though we dared not name for what.
Your dreams, when they came,
were of travel, flight,

lost luggage,
missed planes—
your journey always
a high thin rope
pulled taut between here
and there.

When it shifted,
I do not know,
but there was a time,
brief,
before your last descent,
when I did not wait,
only sat breathing
into that forward motion
of your life,

of mine.

Threshold

Now,
four years later,
this comes to me
complete,
as if I could again
this moment walk
into that house
and you would be there
asking me to turn and walk
again into the room,
across the creaking
floorboard
to your bed—

That one,
right there,
hear how it sings?

You named the notes,
which ones I don't recall,
only that simple joy—
no,
nothing was simple
in your life,
held together by tubes
and the crisscross
of pain
and relief
from pain—

but joy nonetheless
in how,
as all else
slipped away,

you had begun
to find the patterns
underneath,
the music
at the threshold.

Waking Before Light

February

There has to be a February,
every year a sinking down below
the frozen surface of your life,
the sky a grey stained
pillow pressing down
and down where everything you've
ever wanted to forget
or hold lies
dormant in your hot red core.

February days so quiet
you hear your blood inside your veins.

And if you try to cheat it,
fill your days and nights with brightly
colored noise, by-pass February
as you might some broken
town you'd just as soon
forget you'd ever seen,
your life creates another one:
last year May, a swollen river
of a month,
I could not lift my head
above its murky surface;
another year it's August melts me down
like asphalt, any road I hope
to travel buckling with its weight.

Every year there has to be a February,
every year, a sinking down.
You might as well use February
in its time.

Pantoum

In her good cloth coat she circles round the pond
three times— no, four—and quickly,
her white scarf flying off behind, as if a leash
held only by the wind.

Three times—no four, and quickly
the geese rise up above the frozen surface,
held only by the wind
and wing, they fly off into sky.

And does she see them as she circles, circles looking inward?
Her white scarf flying off behind, as if a leash
holds fast her body only—spirit taking flight as
in her good cloth coat she circles round the pond.

Happiness

Happiness
is usually a random occurrence,
a casual twist of the dial—
you never know

what might suddenly lift
up through your body,
once sodden as clay
and heavy with row upon row

of obligation and unfinished thought—
and now you are simply
atom and hope,
your feet rising up through your shoes.

Maybe it's how a temporary shaft
of sun edges in through your window,
a dusty corner
now laced with light,

or a flock of birds overhead
emerging from distant specks of black,
to be feather and caw
and flapping wing,

or maybe it is none of this,
no movement outside yourself at all—
still bare branch
on February sky—

but only a rising up
through some center of yourself
so deep you know your body
must be seven stories underground,

rising, rising, breaking
free without the benefit of beak or wing,
simply rising up and taking flight
within the great expanse of yourself

for a while.

Spring

I wanted a poem
about spring
just beginning to edge its way
up through brown earth's
invisible cracks.

But it came too soon,
this spring.
There were yellow aconite
and crocus,
the first daffodil,

as always,
but suddenly
and all at once:
magnolia, tulip,
lilac buds

and the small brown ants
in their sidewalk cafes,
birds at my morning window.
The poem
I would have written

lay lost
in that gap
between seasons
when the trees barely
shimmered with green.

When there only were
forsythia,
wild onion,

ornamental pear,
I thought that I might

write it still
the way you dream a place
a week or so past leaving,
finish a half-forgotten
conversation with your host—

but redbud interrupted
and the buzzing
of last summer's fly
between the window
and the screen.

This poem needed
silence—
damp dark,
green life emerging,
a world caught nearly unaware.

Loretto Woods

Yesterday I sat
here, at forest's edge
watching day give way to night.
Evening does not fall
but seeps up
from beneath the forest floor,
rising damp and thick as if from
leaf mulch
pushing up and then away
the sounds of rustling leaves and bird song—
now peeper, cricket, frog.

The woods themselves grow larger.
This pond all day
holds sky and bird and life below;
at dusk holds only forest and the night.

Today I sit again,
the water bright with sun,
and all around,
the buzz of wasp and dragonfly.
Overhead a hawk
beats silent wings, then glides
a circle dance around his land,
its boundaries ley lines
he alone can see.

No need to look
for deeper meaning in this day,
no metaphor, no larger story unfolding:
water, sky, earth,
beating wings.
It is enough,
day into night,
day again.

Before the Rain

Morning trees:
still-life lush on greying sky
outside my window.

Before the rain
bird songs hush to necessary
notes.

Even words
moving between mind and pen—
too much noise.

Encounter

She sees me first
and if I am alone,
the soft brown fur
on my neck rises.
Sudden wind
blows through the woods,
I raise my eyes
to hers.

For a moment nothing moves.

Sometimes,
caught there in my gaze,
she calls to those who would
come forward,
her voice pushed up
from somewhere dark and mute:
so much like my own voice rising,
strange and toneless,
from the humus of black dreams.

Why does my heart beat wildly?
I am the only danger here.

Walk

In these dreams
I can get there by walking.
This is important.
I know the way,
though it is far
and I have not walked
there from here before.
I know what streets to take,
when to cut through woods
down the wide ravine
and back among the houses.
But half way there
I begin to remember:
once I passed this tree,
I know this house,
the stone wall there.
And my dreaming self
recalls my dreaming self,
the slap of shoe on wet pavement.

But that was in
another story,
another season,
maybe spring,
the yellow blossoms
frozen to grey sky.

Now it is fall,
the sky as gold
as a light in my window,
and I must
walk and walk,
knowing only
to go on from here,
knowing only that my legs
will carry me
home.

Waking Before Light

There is only shadow,

no sky, no tree, no ground,
no pond beyond.
This window glass
reflects only inward:
the light by my bed, the white mug
in my hand, my face
sharp-shadowed by sleep.

Wait.

Now, not light, not yet,
but a leaching off of darkness
as shadow shapes
itself into branch and leaf,
trunk and limb.
Below, the pond has
pulled itself from ground:
and there is earth and water,
tree and sky,
each in its own place.

Wait.

The sky divides itself again,
a blue below, a blue above,
a band of amber fading
slowly into milky gold,
and now inside this pane of glass
I cannot see
my own sharp face, my pallid light,

but only tree and pond,
and rising from the ground,
fog blue as smoke.

  Somewhere beyond this fog,
  beyond the hills,
  maybe some other
  woman sits beside a window
  or stands in tall wet grass,
  her morning come,
  disk of crimson pushing
  up though earth or water.
  Still,
I wait

till colors pale,
birds fly out from trees,
and sliding now through
edge of sky and earth,
smoke and light,

there is day.

Writing Lessons
(II.)

You really only need to breathe,
as long as you breathe
with everything,

the way your hand breathes in
the shape of a baby's head
as you cradle the soft

green scent of his neck,
and your ears breathe in the teeming
silence of the forest's edge,

and how your eyes breathe in the day
as it cracks wider open
all the way until you see

its fiery center
pushing out the night,
and how your very heart

breathes all you
cannot bear to know
with eyes or ears or skin alone.

Breathe in and hold until your
center burns and swells
but does not crack.

Breathe out.